Faith to Move Mountains

The Power of Intercessory Prayer

the WORD among us

The Word Among Us Press

9639 Doctor Perry Road

Ijamsville, Maryland 21754

ISBN: 0-932085-23-7

© 1999 by The Word Among Us Press

All rights reserved.

Cover design by David Crosson

No part of this publication may be reproduced, stored in a retrieval system, or transmitted in any form or by any means—electronic, mechanical, photocopy, recording, or any other— except for brief quotations in printed reviews, without the prior permission of the publisher.

Made and printed in the United States of America.

Contents

Introduction
4

Portraits of Mary in the Gospels
7

Mary's Journey of Faith
19

Chosen Daughter of Israel
31

Pilgrimage of Faith
43

The Prayer of the Virgin Mary
45

Introduction

How many times have you asked God for something and yet not seen the answer? We seem to have become accustomed to returning from prayer empty-handed. Doesn't our loving God hear us? Doesn't the heavenly Father care about our every need and our every concern? Yes, despite our weakness and sin, our God loves his people deeply and wants to answer their prayers!

In spite of the many trials and difficulties that St. Paul experienced, he knew the power of intercessory prayer. "He who did not spare his own Son but gave him up for us all, will he not also give us all things with him?" (Romans 8:32). Paul interceded for the life of a young boy and witnessed his resurrection (Acts 20:9-12). He was burdened in prayer that the Gentiles would know the gospel, and he witnessed miraculous conversions throughout the Roman empire.

As we intercede and call upon the power of God, we too can see miracles happen. Physical and spiritual wounds can be healed; family relationships can be restored; ethnic violence can melt under the rain of God's peace; bigotry can be erased by love; and apathy can be transformed into a burning fire for the gospel. When our faith unleashes the power of God, every single mountain of sin and suffering can be moved!

As you intercede, don't worry if you feel you lack faith. You may not know what to pray for, but the Holy Spirit, who lives in your heart, will guide your me according to your word." As this prayer flows from our hearts, we can imagine our Father smiling upon us, just as he rejoiced in Mary's words to the angel.

Jeff Smith
The Word Among Us

Portraits of Mary in the Gospels

by

Fr. Joseph F. Wimmer, O.S.A.

When the Son of God entered the world, he didn't simply appear one day in a blaze of glory, bringing salvation the instant he appeared. No, in God's perfect plan, his Son was "born of woman, born under the law, to redeem those who were under the law, so that we might receive adoption as sons" (Galatians 4:4-5). In this book, we look at the life of Mary, the "woman" destined by God to bring his Son into the world. Of all the sons and daughters of Israel, she was destined to be the vessel of the Lord because of her humility and growing desire to see the Lord bring salvation to the earth.

prayer, we have a weapon that has "divine power to destroy strongholds" (2 Corinthians 10:4).

In the following chapters, we will examine this power of intercessory prayer and the effects it can have in our lives and in the world around us. As you read this book, ask the Lord to expand your vision of your inheritance in Christ. Try spending a little time each day praying for your friends, for the church, and for the world. Ask the Spirit to help you pray in union with the mind of God (Romans 8:26-28). Above all, ask the Lord to give you confidence that he hears your prayers and longs to answer the deep needs of those around you. We have a loving God, and he wants us to invite him into every area of our lives.

Loving Our Neighbor Through Prayer. There are many ways to love our neighbor, but intercessory prayer—praying on behalf of other people—should be central to all our efforts. Prayer is the most potent force known to humanity, and the Old Testament provides powerful portraits of intercessors whose examples can teach us and encourage us. These intercessors sought first and foremost to understand God's mind and his will. They waited upon the Spirit and pondered God's word until they knew how to pray and what to pray for.

These heroes and heroines of Israel surrendered their own ideas and desires in favor of God's purposes. They placed more confidence in God's words to them than in their own opinions or the opinions of others. They humbly sought to obey God, often in the face of ridicule and opposition. In the end, they testified to the fact that the prayer of the righteous is powerful and effective (James 5:16-18). Let's take a sage, as Jesus was teaching a crowd gathered around him, he was told that his mother and other relatives were outside, asking for him. Jesus responded: "Who are my mother and my brothers? . . . Here are my mother and my brothers! Whoever does the will of God is my brother, and sister, and mother" (3:33-35).

Jesus' answer, shocking at first, reveals the essence of discipleship—and places Mary at the heart of this calling. She was the first one to "do the will of God," saying to the angel, "Let it be to me according to your word" (Luke 1:38). This simple statement—Mary's *Fiat*—was her life-long disposition.

In the second account, Jesus was rejected in his home town of Nazareth. His former neighbors, scandalized at his new ministry, asked one another: "Where did this man get all this? . . . Is not this the carpenter, the son of Mary?" (Mark 6:2-3). Mark continues: "He could do no mighty work there. . . . And he marveled because of their unbelief" (6:5-6). This story deals primarily with the disbelief of potential disciples, but Mark also gives us insight into Jesus' hidden life. The "son of Mary" was thought of only as a humble carpenter. He was not known for miracles and wondrous deeds, but simply as just another Nazarene. This scene helps us to understand why some people may be disturbed by the way Jesus seemed to respond to Mary in their previous encounter. Only as our hearts are set on God's kingdom—as Mary's heart was—can we come to see who Jesus really is.

In both scenes, Mary was humble and quiet. Her special dignity was veiled, even when her call to discipleship was clearly indicated. This first of disciples remained hidden, seeking no glory or attention. Her only joy was in doing God's will with a humble, loving heart.

Matthew: Mary in the Holy Family. Matthew's Gospel, written around 85 A.D. (perhaps in Syria) for a mostly Jewish-Christian audience, focuses on the formation he confessed his own sins as well as the sins of his people. He united his prayer with all other servants of God and recalled God's promises. Finally, he asked God to grant him favor in the eyes of the king of Babylon so that he would be permitted to return to Jerusalem and rebuild the city. Upon arriving in Jerusalem, Nehemiah was confronted with tremendous adversity. Still, his devotion to his people, coupled with the grace of intercessory prayer, cleared the way for God to use him powerfully in the restoration of the Jewish people.

Habakkuk: Taking Up a "Burden". Although it is only three chapters long, the book of Habakkuk provides a wonderfully clear portrait of someone who learned how to intercede. The book is short enough to be read in one sitting, which is probably the best way to understand Habakkuk's intercession. We will focus on only a few excerpts to give you a glimpse of Habakkuk's zeal for seeking and praying according to the mind of God.

The oracle of God which Habakkuk the prophet saw. (Habakkuk 1:1)

The very first verse indicates that an intercessor is one who takes up a burden that goes far beyond his or her own needs and intentions. Habakkuk lived between the late seventh and early sixth centuries before Christ, a time of spiritual, moral, and political decline for Jerusalem. The prophet was deeply wounded in conscience by the violence and oppression that surrounded him—how his fellow Israelites seemed to have total disregard for the Lord and his commandments. In grief over his people's condition, Habakkuk cried out to the Lord, pouring out his

Jesus and Joseph, Luke captures her status as virgin mother of the incarnate God. Of all four gospels, there is something special in Luke's portrayal of Mary. He seems to penetrate her character and show us more of her human qualities, attributes which could guide us as well: her humility, generosity, faith, and joy; her life of prayer; her maternal instincts.

When she heard about her older cousin Elizabeth's pregnancy, Mary "went with haste" to her side, to share her joy and to be of service (Luke 1:39). When Elizabeth praised her faith, Mary replied with the Magnificat, that beautiful hymn which glorified the Lord's holiness, justice, and mercy (1:46-55). Like Hannah of old (1 Samuel 1-2), Mary recognized that despite her "low estate," all generations would call her blessed because of the great things the Lord had done in her (Luke 1:48-49). Humility always acknowledges the truth—even of one's own blessedness—a central theme in Luke (see 10:19-20).

At Bethlehem, Mary gave birth to Jesus, tenderly caring for his needs even despite their lack of almost everything (Luke 2:7). When the shepherds arrived and spoke of an angel's announcement of the Messiah's birth, Mary "kept all these things, pondering them in her heart" (2:19). This prayerful disposition no doubt prepared her to receive Simeon's words, at Jesus' presentation in the temple: "A sword will pierce through your own soul also" (2:35).

When Mary and Joseph found the twelve-year-old Jesus in the temple, it was Mary who took the initiative to express her concern: "Son, why have you treated us so? Your father and I have been looking for you anxiously" (Luke 2:48). Even when Jesus explained himself, they did not understand his words, but Mary "kept all these things in her heart"(2:50-51). This was probably one of the key moments when Mary had to face the implications of her "yes" to the angel at the annunciation. Here, twelve years later, Mary had the

A Union of Wills. Habakkuk waited patiently, and eventually received a reply. Not only did God answer his questions, he also told the prophet to write down the revelation and make it known. Because he interceded by humbly waiting on God, Habakkuk became a spiritual father to the people of Jerusalem, offering prophetic words of warning and encouragement to God's children. What was the answer Habakkuk received?

He whose soul is not upright in him shall fail, but the righteous shall live by his faith. (Habakkuk 2:4)

Habakkuk understood that his people were about to experience the catastrophe of enemy occupation, the destruction of their temple, and exile. He saw that God was bringing his people into a situation so traumatic that they would not be able to think, manipulate, or bully their way out of it. They would mystery of Jesus in all its profound depth and glory. John speaks of Mary only twice, once toward the beginning of his gospel and once toward the end—at Cana (John 2:1-12) and at the foot of the cross (19:26-27). In both scenes, Mary was involved in the lives of others besides Jesus, but always in union with him.

At Cana Mary told Jesus, "They have no wine." Though his answer seems to rebuke her, she confidently instructed the stewards: "Do whatever he tells you" (2:3,5). Evidently, Jesus' hour had arrived, occasioned by Mary's intercession and persevering faith. By turning the water into wine, Jesus created a powerful symbol of his message, that the reign of God was being inaugurated as a joyful messianic banquet. All this at Mary's initiative!

When Jesus—on the cross—told the beloved disciple, "Behold, your mother" (19:26-27), he was entrusting Mary to this disciple's care, but as a "mother." This unnamed beloved disciple represents the whole Christian community, and so at her son's request, Mary became mother of the church. As a mother, Mary is a new Eve, for in both scenes she was addressed as "woman" (2:4; 19:26), an allusion to the "woman" at Adam's side (Genesis 2:23), "the mother of all living" (Genesis 3:20).

A Mirror of the Mystery. Mary's person and vocation mirror the mystery of Jesus and the mystery of our own lives. Like Mary, we too are disciples called to follow Jesus in faith, love, and service. By telling her story in four different ways, the gospels give us a multi-faceted view of the richness of her life and all that she offers to the church. Whether we see her as the first disciple, as a member of the holy family, as virgin mother of God incarnate, or as mother of the church, we can honor and admire her, follow her counsels, and call her sister, mother, and friend.

Mary's Journey of Faith

by

Jeff Smith

So many paintings and sculptures portray Mary kneeling, with her hands folded and head bowed, prayerful and peaceful. These artworks seek to convey the sense of serenity that we often associate with the Mother of God, a peace that came from quietly treasuring and pondering God's actions in her heart (Luke 2:19).

Yet as quiet as Mary must have been, she was also active, questioning, growing, and learning. From the moment of the angel's visit, Mary began a journey of faith that brought her to an ever deeper experience of

God's love. Every challenge, every obstacle, every threat to her peace, gave her the opportunity to trust God more completely and to allow the Spirit to pour more love into her heart. Mary never drew back from these challenges, but allowed them to form her more and more into the vessel of grace that she was destined to become.

In this chapter, we examine Mary's journey of faith, looking at the way she responded to the challenges placed before her. The more we come to understand how the Spirit moved her and formed her, the more we can understand the Spirit's actions in our own lives. Just as Mary grew through her obedience and love for God, the Spirit wants to form these same dispositions in our hearts.

An Open Heart. Growing up in Palestine in the first century B.C., Mary would have joined her people in praying for the coming Messiah and the fulfillment of God's promises. She doubtless heard some of her fellow

Jews crying out for deliverance, not only from Roman domination, but from the divisions among their own people as well. She would have prayed for the restoration of Zion, the holy city of Yahweh, as the gathering place of the chosen people. Listening to the Hebrew scripture must have filled her heart with a deep longing and with the faith that God would not abandon his people. In so many ways, Mary's heart seemed ripe to receive the good news.

Yet scripture tells us that when Gabriel appeared to her, Mary was "greatly troubled" by his greeting (Luke 1:29). The angel went on to tell her that she was to conceive miraculously and bear a child who would be called "holy, the Son of God" (1:35). This child would "save his people from their sins" (Matthew 1:21). Despite all the preparation in Mary's heart—even despite her sinless purity—the angel's appearance disturbed Mary and confronted her with an unexpected challenge. She was being invited by Almighty God to participate in his plan of salvation, and in a way marvelous beyond imagining!

Mary could not grasp why God would choose a lowly, uneducated girl like herself to fulfill such a mission. And even though she was probably familiar with Isaiah's words that a virgin would conceive and bear a child called Immanuel—"God with us"—the notion that she would conceive by the power of the Spirit was still too incredible to grasp.

While Mary's mind could not fully grasp this revelation, her faith and love for God enabled her to say yes. Despite the fear, the uncertainty about the future, and the many questions that must have entered her mind, Mary knew in her heart that God was trustworthy. This humble "handmaid of the Lord" (Luke 1:38) chose to remain faithful to God. As the angel left her, Mary's journey of faith entered a new era. She began an adventure that was to surpass anything she could have envisioned.

Pondering and Treasuring. We can trace Mary's journey of faith by looking at the different journeys she made during her life. Once the angel left her, Mary "went with haste into the hill country, to a city of Judah" (Luke 1:39), to visit Elizabeth, her kinswoman, who had conceived the herald of the Messiah. It was at least a three-day journey, and so Mary must have had plenty of time to think and pray. We can picture her recalling her encounter with the angel again and again, as the Spirit prepared her heart more deeply for her newly revealed role in God's plan. When she arrived at Elizabeth's home, her prayer of praise and gratitude—the Magnificat—welled up from a heart that had been deeply touched by the Spirit (1:47-55).

Luke often portrays Mary quietly pondering the things that she witnessed and treasuring them in her heart (see Luke 1:29; 2:19,51). This was not an anxiety-laden attempt to make sense out of confusing circumstances. Rather, faced with events too wondrous for her mind to grasp, Mary turned to God for understanding. Even as she gave serious thought to what had happened, she opened her heart to the Lord and asked him to teach her more about this Messiah, conceived by the Spirit, who was to be her son. As a result, even as Jesus was physically growing in Mary's womb, he was also growing in her heart.

Preparation and Testing. As the time for Jesus' birth drew near, the Lord began to show Mary what kind of reception the world would provide for her son. While there could have been numerous reasons why "there was no place for them in the inn" at Bethlehem (Luke 2:7), Luke paints this scene to foreshadow the rejection that Jesus would face throughout his earthly life. The eternal Son of God was born in a state of poverty, unnoticed by the rich and powerful. Angels heralded his birth, but only to "unimportant" shepherds. From the very start, Jesus was welcomed by the humble and opposed by the powerful.

At the time of Jesus' presentation in the temple, Mary received a foretaste of her own participation in Jesus' rejection. The aged Simeon—who had longed eagerly to see the promised Messiah—prophesied that Jesus was destined to be a "sign that is spoken against." And in the next breath, he told Mary "and a sword will pierce through your own soul" (Luke 2:34-35). Jesus' mission was to be filled with controversy, rejection, and sorrow, and Mary—his first disciple—would share in his suffering. At the very beginning of her life as the mother of the Christ, Mary faced the mystery of the cross. The redemption she longed and prayed for would not come about peacefully; it would cost her and her son dearly.

The signs of Jesus' rejection increased as time went on. In order to avoid Herod's murderous rage, Mary and Joseph had to flee to Egypt (Matthew 2:13-15). They became refugees, exiles from their homeland, retracing the journey of the children of Israel who fled Pharaoh's wrath. In her flight, Mary faced another stage in her journey—a more difficult one. He who had visited her so graciously through the angel was now testing and strengthening her faith, calling her to a deeper trust in him. Mary was growing in a strength that comes from humbly surrendering one's heart to the Lord and prayerfully pondering his word.

During the "hidden years" prior to Jesus' public ministry, Mary's love for God would have deepened as she taught her son about Simeon's prophecy, about the circumstances surrounding his birth, and the angel's words to her. Through all these years, as she and Joseph taught and formed the child, the Spirit was at work in Mary, clarifying her understanding of who Jesus was. In prayer, she pondered again and again the scriptural promises; she asked God for wisdom; and she closely observed her son—the Son of God—as he grew strong in the Spirit and approached the time of his ministry.

The Time is Fulfilled. The Gospel of John surrounds Jesus' public ministry with two events involving Mary. At the wedding feast of Cana (John 2:1-11), Jesus seemed reluctant at first to perform any miracles. But his mother's heart—her disposition of faith and trust—moved him to begin his ministry. Mary's intercession shows how her faith had deepened and matured beyond that of the apostles, who had not yet been tested as she had. In humility, she persisted in prayerful expectancy that God would grant her heart's desire—a wonderful sign of the coming kingdom.

At Cana, Mary showed more than just her compassion for the couple whose nuptial celebration was threatened. She had begun to understand her son's mission and was eager for his work to begin. Years earlier, the angel had told her that Jesus would inherit the kingdom of David (Luke 1:32-33); now she longed to see this kingdom come. While Jesus knew it was not yet the "hour" (when he would be glorified on the cross—John 2:4), he yielded to her request, performing a miracle that pointed to the longing in both their hearts for the eternal "wedding banquet." What hope Mary must have drawn from this sign, even as she learned to trust her son more deeply!

Mary was also present at the end of Jesus' ministry—on Calvary, where she experienced the fulfillment of Simeon's prophecy (John 19:25-27). As she watched her son's agony, did the angel's hopeful promises seem meaningless and empty to her? Jesus was supposed to be "great . . . the Son of the Most High. . . . Of his kingdom there [would] be no end" (Luke 1:32-33). How was she to understand this? "Standing at the foot of the cross, Mary is the witness, humanly speaking, of the complete negation of these words." Yet, "How completely she abandons herself to

God without reserve" (John Paul II, *Mother of the Redeemer*, 18).

Mary's journey of faith had taken her down roads she never expected to travel and, with each passing year, her faith deepened. Through trials and through joys, she watched the Father's plan unfold, and she willingly played the part God had marked out for her. Even though her heart was pierced with anguish at her son's death, she never once cursed God or abandoned her calling. Even as she held her son's dead body, Mary knew that it must be this way, and that this man's death effected the greatest of all miracles—humanity's reconciliation with God. Now, the kingdom she longed for had come, and she had only to wait for Easter Sunday to see all her hopes fulfilled and her sorrows reversed.

The Mirror of Faith. Even though she played a special role in God's loving plan, Mary remained a humble, lowly believer. From her conception she was graced with the merits of Jesus' cross—freedom from the bondage of sin. Yet she still faced real, human choices and felt real, human emotions. Her triumph was a triumph of faith—the same faith available to each of us.

God invites all of us on a pilgrimage of faith. He wants all of us to treasure his voice in our hearts, to ponder his word in scripture. Mary has given us a beautiful example of what it means to yield to God. She has taught us to listen to God's voice and to allow the Holy Spirit to guide us. May her prayer burn in our hearts as well: "Behold the servant of the Lord; let it be done to me according to your word."

Chosen Daughter of Israel

by

Jeff Smith

In the eternal counsels of the Trinity, before anything was created—even before time itself began—a plan was established. God's plan encompassed everything that was to be created, including every person on the face of the earth. As the letter to the Ephesians proclaims, God has "blessed us in Christ with every spiritual blessing in the heavenly places" (Ephesians 1:3). The letter goes on to say that God "chose us in him before the foundation of the world, that we should be holy and blameless before him" (1:4), and that he "destined us in love to be his sons through Jesus Christ" (1:5).

This wondrous plan—that we would all be filled with divine life and become beloved sons and daughters of God—is at the heart of everything God has done. It is so central that not even our fall into sin could destroy it. God so wanted us to share in his life that he offered up his only Son to bring us back to him (John 3:16). Each of us has been chosen in Christ, destined to be filled with his love and to fulfill a specific role in his kingdom. Mary's role—because it is so pivotal to the coming of redemption—stands as an example for us of the wonderful things that can happen to us as we yield to the Lord in our hearts and allow him to unfold his plan for our lives—just as he did for Mary.

Pope John Paul II wrote that "in the mystery of Christ [Mary] is present even 'before the creation of the world,' as the one whom the Father 'has chosen' " (Mother of the Redeemer, 8). Imagine how important the character of the mother of the Son of God must be.

She was destined to be more than simply the vessel through which the Son would enter the world. Both in her heart and in her deeds she was chosen to sum up Israel's centuries-old longing for God's promises to be fulfilled. She was destined to give birth to, nurture, and train the one who would save all people from sin! God intended that she would become the model for all Christians throughout the centuries—showing by her example and helping to effect by her intercession the purity of heart and singleness of mind that God desires in all his children.

The Link between the Old and New Testament. Faithful to his chosen people, God destined that the Messiah would come through a daughter of Israel, one freed from the taint of original sin. He intended that the mother of the Redeemer be a humble woman who would not seek attention from the world. She was to be one of the "poor," trusting completely in God, perfectly fulfilling the law which Moses had given to her ancestors on Mount Sinai.

The Gospel of Luke gives special insight into Mary's role as a faithful daughter of Israel. Luke places Mary in the tradition of Israelite women that included Abraham's wife Sarah (Genesis 18:1-15; 21:1-7); the unnamed mother of Samson (Judges 13:2-5,24); and Hannah, Samuel's mother (1 Samuel 1:1-2,9-20). Each of these women conceived miraculously and gave birth to men of God who, each in his own way, foreshadowed Christ, both in his character and his mission. Summing up and giving even greater meaning to all these miracles, Mary bore Jesus, the Savior in whom all of God's promises are fulfilled.

Matthew makes explicit reference to Isaiah's prophecy that a virgin (or "young woman") would conceive and bear a son called Immanuel (Isaiah 7:14; Matthew 1:23). In Isaiah's time, the prophecy about Immanuel was taken to mean the still unborn heir of

Ahaz, king of Judah, who would protect the country from foreign invasion. The first Christians, however, saw in this prophecy Mary, a virginal young woman, who would conceive miraculously and bring the Son of God himself into our midst. In the fullness of time, Jesus became the true Immanuel—God with us.

Finally, the book of Revelation speaks of a woman in labor whose unborn child is threatened by a dragon, or a serpent (Revelation 12:1-9). When the child is born, he is safely taken up to the throne of God, while the woman flees into the wilderness. Many believers through the centuries have come to see this woman as Mary, the new Eve, whose offspring would triumph over the ancient serpent whose deception led humanity into sin (see Genesis 3:15-16). In all these traditions, we see Mary's role foreshadowed. This chosen daughter of Zion, humbly submitted to the Spirit, brought forth the Savior, Israel's greatest longing, the one for whom God had prepared so long.

The Fulfillment of the Times. Through these ties with the Old Testament, we can begin to understand Mary's role in the history of Israel. She would have been intimately familiar with God's promises concerning the Messiah, and like her people, she hungered for this Messiah to come and redeem Israel. How fervently she must have prayed with her fellow Israelites, "How long, O Lord?" (Psalm 13:1; see also 90:13), waiting and hoping for the promised salvation!

When the angel invited Mary to participate in God's plan in such an unexpected manner, her longing for the Messiah moved her to yield freely. In her *Fiat*—"Let it be to me according to your word" (Luke 1:38)—this daughter of Israel inaugurated a new era in God's design. His promised redemption—the new, unbreakable covenant—was to be finally brought to pass. In Mary's womb, her people's longing for Christ was fulfilled.

Even as she stood at the cross, watching her son die an agonizing death, Mary was in a privileged position.

Her heart was pierced with a sword, just as Simeon had prophesied (Luke 2:35), but she also sensed that something momentous was occurring. All the years of prayer and openness to the Spirit had taught her that this man's death would bring life to the world. More than anyone else present on Calvary, she was able to see through the sorrow and see the redemption. All of mankind's sin was being wiped away before her very eyes. The Father's love was being released in a new and definitive way. Redemption had come, and she was privileged to witness it—greatly though it cost her.

Mother of the Church. Mary not only witnessed the miracle of the cross, she was also present on the day of Pentecost. There, in the upper room, the age of the church was inaugurated, the final era before Jesus' return. All throughout this age—particularly in the past two centuries—Mary continues to fulfill God's purposes for her. Just as she did at Cana, she continues to intercede with her son. In addition, she shows her concern through various apparitions, in which the Mother of God speaks to the children of God. Whether the messages concern turning away from sin or experiencing God's love in prayer, these apparitions seem to focus on preparing the world for Jesus' return at the end of time.

Catherine and Bernadette: The Grace of the Lord. For example, when she appeared to Catherine Labouré in 1830, Mary spoke a two-fold message of grace and judgment: "My child, the times are very evil. Sorrows will befall France; the throne will be overturned. The whole world will be plunged into every kind of misery. But come to the foot of the altar. There graces will be shed upon all, great and small, who ask for them. Especially will graces be shed upon those who ask for them."

Recounting her later vision of the Miraculous Medal, Catherine said: "It made me realize how right it was to pray to the Blessed Virgin and how generous she was to those who did pray to her, what graces she gave to those who asked for them, what joy she had in giving them." Just as she willingly directed the stewards at Cana toward her son (John 2:5), so even now Mary rejoices in leading God's people back to him.

We can also see Mary's eagerness to bring people to the Lord in the story of Bernadette at Lourdes. From the time when she appeared there in 1858 to the present, countless people have flocked to this little French village to seek the Lord's healing touch. Thousands of lame, blind, and deaf pilgrims have been healed there, and many more have been brought to conversion and a deeper experience of God's love.

Fatima: Intercession and Repentance. As the humble daughter of Israel who longed for the Messiah to come, Mary continues to pray—and invite others to pray with her—that many people would turn to the

Lord through repentance and faith. In 1917—during World War I—Mary appeared to nine-year-old Lucia Abobora and her two younger cousins in Fatima, Portugal, to urge them to pray for those lost in sin. In one vision, Mary showed the children the pain and anguish experienced by those in hell. They were like "coals in a fiery furnace, with never an instant's peace or freedom."

In her final message—on October 13, 1917—Mary told the children: "People must amend their lives, ask pardon for their sins, and not offend our Lord any more, for he is already too greatly offended." In all her appearances to them, Mary urged the children to pray for the world, that many would be saved from sin as they repent and put their faith in her son.

Thy Kingdom Come. There have been many other times when people have attested to seeing Mary, including La Salette (France) in 1846, Knock (Ireland) in 1879, Beauraing (Belgium) in 1932, and Medjugorje (Yugoslavia-Croatia) from 1981 to the present. What stands out in all these appearances is Mary's longing for all people to be prepared for Jesus' second coming. She has often appeared with tears, weeping over the sin in the world and imploring people to repent and to seek her son in prayer.

Destined from before all time to be the Mother of God, Mary continues to invite every disciple of Jesus to follow her example. As Jesus' first disciple, she prayed: "Let it be done to me according to your word." This prayer—which most clearly reveals Mary's heart—is a prayer each of us can learn to say with ever-increasing trust. Through the power of the Spirit, we can begin to long for Jesus to come again, just as Mary prayed centuries ago for his first appearance. We too have been destined from the beginning of time; we too are his dearly beloved sons and daughters. With hope and confidence, let us take up our mission on earth as we await the coming kingdom and the full unveiling of the Father's plan for every man and woman.

A Pilgrimage of Faith

From the moment of the Annunciation and conception, from the moment of his birth in the stable at Bethlehem, Mary followed Jesus step by step in her maternal pilgrimage of faith. She followed him during the years of his hidden life at Nazareth; she followed him also during the time after he left home, when he began "to do and to teach" (Acts 1:1) in the midst of Israel. Above all she followed him in the tragic experience of Golgotha.

Now, while Mary was with the apostles in the upper room in Jerusalem at the dawn of the church, her faith, born from the words of the Annunciation, found confirmation. The angel had said to her then: "You will conceive in your womb and bear a son. . . . And of his kingdom there will be no end." The recent events on Calvary had shrouded that promise in darkness, yet not even beneath the cross did Mary's faith fail. She had still remained the one who, like Abraham, "in hope believed against hope" (Romans 4:18).

But it is only after the resurrection that hope had shown its true face and the promise had begun to be transformed into reality. For Jesus, before returning to the Father, had said to the Apostles: "Go therefore and make disciples of all nations . . . lo, I am with you always, to the close of the age" (Matthew 28:19-20). Thus had spoken the one who by his resurrection had revealed himself as the conqueror of death, as the one who possessed the kingdom of which, as the angel said, "there will be no end."

(Pope John Paul II, *Mother of the Redeemer*, 27)

The Prayer of the Virgin Mary

Mary's prayer is revealed to us at the dawning of the fullness of time. Before the incarnation of the Son of God, and before the outpouring of the Holy Spirit, her prayer cooperates in a unique way with the Father's plan of loving kindness: at the Annunciation, for Christ's conception; at Pentecost, for the formation of the Church, his Body. In the faith of his humble handmaid, the Gift of God found the acceptance he had awaited from the beginning of time. She whom the Almighty made "full of grace" responds by offering her whole being: "Behold I am the handmaid of the Lord; let it be [done] to me according to your word." "*Fiat*": this is Christian prayer: to be wholly God's because he is wholly ours.

The Gospel reveals to us how Mary prays and intercedes in faith. At Cana, the mother of Jesus asks her son for the needs of a wedding feast; this is the sign of another feast—that of the wedding of the Lamb where he gives his body and blood at the request of the Church, his Bride. It is at the hour of the New Covenant, at the foot of the cross, that Mary is heard as the Woman, the new Eve, the true "mother of all the living."

That is why the Canticle of Mary, the *Magnificat* (Latin) or *Megalynei* (Byzantine) is the song both of the Mother of God and of the Church; the song of the Daughter of Zion and of the new People of God; the song of thanksgiving for the fullness of graces poured out in the economy of salvation and the song of the "poor" whose hope is met by the fulfillment of the promises made to our ancestors, "to Abraham and to his posterity for ever."

Catechism of the Catholic Church, 2617-2619